I0012343

The Fiverr

Freelancer's

Handbook:

Tips, Tricks, and Strategies for
Success

ABOUT

In this comprehensive handbook, you'll learn the ins and outs of the Fiverr platform, including how to create a winning profile, find and bid on jobs, and manage client relationships.

BG PUBLISHING

TABLE OF CONTENTS

Chapter 1: Introduction to Freelancing on Fiverr

- Explanation of what Fiverr is and how it works
- Overview of the benefits and challenges of freelancing on Fiverr

If you're considering freelancing as a way to make money, Fiverr is an excellent place to start. Fiverr is one of the most popular and user-friendly platforms for freelancers, offering a wide variety of services and opportunities to connect with clients from all over the world.

In this chapter, we'll provide you with a comprehensive overview of Fiverr and how it works. We'll also walk you through the steps you need to take to set up your Fiverr account and start selling your services.

What is Fiverr?

Fiverr is an online marketplace that connects freelancers with clients who are looking for specific services. Freelancers create profiles on the platform and offer "gigs" - services that they can provide to clients for a fee. Clients can then search for freelancers who offer the services they need and hire them directly through the Fiverr platform.

Getting Started on Fiverr

To get started on Fiverr, you'll need to create a freelancer account. This is a simple process that requires you to provide some basic information about yourself and your services. Once you've created your account, you can start setting up your profile, which is essentially your storefront on Fiverr.

Your profile should showcase your skills and experience and give potential clients a sense of who you are and what you can do. You can include a profile picture, a description of your services, and samples of your work.

Finding Work on Fiverr

Once your profile is set up, you can start looking for work on Fiverr. There are several ways to do this, including:

- Browsing the Fiverr marketplace: You can search for gigs in your area of expertise and bid on them directly through the platform.

- Responding to buyer requests: Clients can post requests for specific services they need, and freelancers can respond with offers to complete the job.
- Promoting your gigs: You can promote your gigs on social media or through other marketing channels to attract clients.

Fiverr is an excellent platform for freelancers who are just starting out, as well as those who are looking to expand their client base and earn more money. In this chapter, we've provided you with an overview of how Fiverr works and how you can get started on the platform. In the following chapters, we'll dive deeper into the strategies and tactics you can use to succeed as a Fiverr freelancer.

Chapter 2: Getting Started as a Freelancer on Fiverr

- Tips for creating a strong Fiverr profile
- How to choose the right niche or specialty for your skills
- Understanding Fiverr's rules and regulations

Now that you have a general understanding of Fiverr and how it works, it's time to dive deeper into what it takes to succeed as a freelancer on the platform. In this chapter, we'll provide you with practical tips and advice for getting started as a Fiverr freelancer.

Niche Down Your Services

One of the keys to success on Fiverr is to niche down your services. Instead of offering a broad range of services, focus on a specific area of expertise. This will help you stand out from the competition and attract clients who are looking for a freelancer with specialized skills.

Set Your Prices

When setting your prices on Fiverr, it's important to be competitive while also valuing your time and expertise. Take some time to research what other freelancers in your niche are charging and adjust your prices accordingly. Remember that Fiverr takes a 20% commission on all orders, so factor that into your pricing strategy.

Craft Your Gig

Descriptions Your gig descriptions are your opportunity to showcase your skills and convince potential clients to hire you. Make sure your descriptions are clear, concise, and compelling. Be sure to include information about the scope of the project, the deliverables you'll provide, and any relevant experience or qualifications you have.

Optimize Your Profile

Your Fiverr profile is like your storefront on the platform. Make sure it's optimized to attract potential clients. Use a professional profile picture, include a detailed description of your services and experience, and showcase your portfolio with relevant samples of your work.

Communicate Effectively with Clients

Communication is key when working with clients on Fiverr. Make sure you respond promptly to messages and keep clients updated on the progress of their project. Be professional and courteous at all times, and don't be afraid to ask for clarification if you're unsure about a client's requirements.

Getting started as a freelancer on Fiverr can be challenging, but with the right strategies and mindset, it's possible to succeed. In this chapter, we've provided you with practical tips and advice for setting up your Fiverr profile, crafting compelling gig descriptions, and communicating effectively with clients. In the next chapter, we'll dive deeper into how to market your services on the platform and attract more clients.

Chapter 3: Setting Prices and Managing Time Effectively

- Strategies for pricing your services competitively and fairly
- Time management techniques for balancing multiple projects

- Tools and apps to help you stay organized and on track

One of the biggest challenges for freelancers on Fiverr is finding the right balance between setting competitive prices and managing their time effectively. In this chapter, we'll explore strategies for setting your prices and managing your time to maximize your earning potential while still maintaining a healthy work-life balance.

Setting Your Prices

Setting your prices on Fiverr can be a tricky balancing act. You want to be competitive enough to attract clients, but you also need to value your time and expertise. Here are some tips for setting your prices:

- Research the competition: Look at what other freelancers in your niche are charging and adjust your prices accordingly.
- Consider your experience: If you're just starting out, you may need to charge lower prices to build up your portfolio and attract clients. As you

gain more experience and positive reviews, you can raise your prices.

- Offer packages: Consider offering packages that include multiple services or a set number of revisions. This can help you earn more while also providing value to your clients.

Managing Your Time

As a freelancer, it can be tempting to work around the clock to meet client deadlines and earn more money. However, it's important to prioritize your time and maintain a healthy work-life balance. Here are some tips for managing your time effectively:

- Set boundaries: Establish clear working hours and stick to them. Communicate your availability to clients and let them know when they can expect to hear back from you.
- Prioritize your workload: Make a to-do list each day and prioritize your tasks

based on their urgency and importance. This will help you stay focused and avoid getting overwhelmed.

- Take breaks: It's important to take breaks throughout the day to recharge and avoid burnout. Take a walk, stretch, or do something else that helps you relax and clear your mind.

Setting your prices and managing your time effectively are crucial components of success as a freelancer on Fiverr. By researching the competition, valuing your expertise, and prioritizing your workload, you can maximize your earning potential while still maintaining a healthy work-life balance. In the next chapter, we'll explore strategies for marketing your services on Fiverr and attracting more clients.

Chapter 4: Communicating Effectively with Clients

- Best practices for understanding client needs and expectations
- How to communicate professionally and respectfully with clients
- Dealing with negative feedback and difficult clients

Clear communication is essential for success as a freelancer on Fiverr. In this chapter, we'll explore strategies for communicating effectively with clients to build strong relationships, avoid misunderstandings, and ensure satisfaction.

Understanding Client Needs

To effectively communicate with your clients, it's important to first understand their needs. Take the time to ask questions, clarify their expectations, and ensure that you fully understand the project requirements before getting started. Here are some tips for understanding client needs:

- Ask questions: Be sure to ask your client any questions you may have about their project requirements, deadlines, and expectations. This will help you deliver the best possible work.

- Repeat back: To avoid misunderstandings, repeat back the project requirements and expectations in your own words to ensure that you've understood everything correctly.
- Listen actively: Be an active listener and pay close attention to what your client is saying. This will help you identify any potential issues or areas where you can provide additional value.

Setting Expectations

Setting clear expectations is crucial for avoiding misunderstandings and ensuring client satisfaction. Here are some tips for setting expectations:

- Define project scope: Clearly define the scope of the project, including what is included and what is not.
- Set realistic deadlines: Be honest about how long the project will take

and set realistic deadlines. If you think you need more time, communicate this with your client upfront.

- Establish communication protocols: Establish clear communication protocols, such as how often you'll provide updates and how you'll communicate throughout the project.

Managing Client Communication

Managing client communication effectively is a key part of success on Fiverr. Here are some tips for managing communication:

- Use a professional tone: Keep your communication professional and courteous, even if the client is difficult.
- Be responsive: Respond to client messages and requests in a timely manner. If you can't respond right away, let them know when they can expect to hear back from you.

- Provide regular updates: Keep your client updated on your progress throughout the project, including any issues or delays.

Effective communication is crucial for success as a freelancer on Fiverr. By understanding client needs, setting clear expectations, and managing client communication effectively, you can build strong relationships with clients and ensure satisfaction. In the next chapter, we'll explore strategies for marketing your services on Fiverr and attracting more clients.

Chapter 5: Building a Client Base and Promoting Your Services

- Techniques for promoting your services and standing out from the competition
- How to build relationships with clients and network with other freelancers
- Tips for creating a professional portfolio and showcasing your work

As a freelancer on Fiverr, building a strong client base is essential for success. In this chapter, we'll explore strategies for promoting your services and attracting more clients.

Creating a Strong Profile

Your Fiverr profile is the first thing potential clients will see when they search for services. A strong profile is key to attracting clients and building your reputation. Here are some tips for creating a strong profile:

- Choose a professional profile picture: Use a professional headshot or logo as your profile picture.
- Write a clear and concise bio: Your bio should clearly describe your services and what makes you unique.
- Showcase your work: Include examples of your work, such as portfolio items or past projects.
- Highlight your skills and experience: Make sure your profile showcases

your skills and experience relevant to the services you offer.

Marketing Your Services

Marketing your services is essential for attracting more clients. Here are some strategies to consider:

- Use keywords: Use relevant keywords in your gig title and description to make it easier for clients to find your services.
- Offer discounts: Consider offering discounts or promotional offers to attract new clients.
- Create social media profiles: Promote your services on social media by creating profiles on relevant platforms and sharing your work.
- Use paid advertising: Consider using paid advertising, such as Google Ads or Facebook Ads, to reach a wider audience.

Managing Your Reputation

Your reputation is everything on Fiverr. Building a positive reputation is key to attracting more clients and growing your business. Here are some tips for managing your reputation:

- Provide high-quality work: Deliver high-quality work and exceed client expectations to earn positive reviews.
- Respond to feedback: Respond to client feedback, both positive and negative, to show that you value their input and are committed to improving your services.
- Be reliable: Meet deadlines and respond to client messages in a timely manner to build a reputation for reliability.
- Go above and beyond: Consider going above and beyond to provide extra value to clients, such as offering additional revisions or providing additional resources.

Building a strong client base and promoting your services is essential for success as a freelancer on Fiverr. By creating a strong profile, marketing your services, and managing your reputation, you can attract more clients and grow your business. In the next chapter, we'll explore strategies for managing your finances and setting goals for your business.

Chapter 6: Managing Financial Aspects of Freelancing

- Overview of tax and financial considerations for freelancers
- Strategies for handling payments, invoices, and contracts
- Tools and resources for managing finances as a freelancer

One of the most important aspects of freelancing is managing your finances effectively. As a freelancer on Fiverr, it's essential to have a clear understanding of how to handle your income, expenses, and taxes. In this chapter, we'll cover some basic financial management tips to help you run your freelancing business successfully.

Section 1: Income and Expenses

- Understanding your income streams as a freelancer

- How to keep track of your income and expenses

- Using tools like spreadsheets or accounting software to manage your finances

- Creating a budget and tracking your expenses to stay on top of your finances

- Identifying tax-deductible expenses to help reduce your taxable income

When freelancing on Fiverr, managing your income and expenses is crucial to your success. As a freelancer, you are responsible for tracking your earnings, paying taxes, and managing your cash flow. This section will cover the basics of income and expenses, including how to track your earnings and expenses, how to set your rates, and how to handle taxes.

Setting Your Rates

One of the most important things to consider as a freelancer on Fiverr is how to set your rates. There are a few things to keep in mind when deciding on your pricing. First, consider your skills and experience. If you are just starting out, you may need to charge lower rates to attract clients. As you gain more experience and build a portfolio, you can raise your rates.

Another factor to consider is the type of work you are offering. Some services may be more specialized and therefore command a higher rate, while others may be more generic and have a lower rate. It's important to research the going rate for similar services on Fiverr to ensure that you are charging a fair price.

Tracking Your Earnings

Once you have set your rates and started working with clients, it's important to track your earnings. This will help you understand your income and how much you are making from your freelancing work. You can track your earnings using tools such as spreadsheets or financial management software. Fiverr also offers a feature that allows you to track your earnings directly within the platform.

Tracking Your Expenses

In addition to tracking your earnings, it's important to track your expenses. This includes any expenses related to your freelancing work, such as equipment or software costs, office expenses, and marketing expenses. By tracking your expenses, you can deduct them from your taxes, which can save you money.

Managing Your Cash Flow

Cash flow management is critical when freelancing on Fiverr. It's important to have a clear understanding of your income and expenses so you can plan accordingly. This includes understanding when payments are due and how long it takes for payments to clear.

In addition to understanding your cash flow, it's important to have a system for invoicing and receiving payments from clients. Fiverr offers a system for invoicing and receiving payments directly within the platform, which can make the process more streamlined and efficient.

In conclusion, managing your income and expenses is critical when freelancing on Fiverr. By setting your rates appropriately, tracking your earnings and expenses, and managing your cash flow, you can build a successful freelance business.

Section 2: Taxes and Legal Considerations

- Understanding your tax obligations as a freelancer

- Registering your business and obtaining any necessary permits or licenses

- Choosing the best legal structure for your business

- Understanding tax deductions and credits for freelancers

- Keeping proper records to make tax time easier

As a freelancer on Fiverr, it is essential to understand the taxes and legal considerations that come with running a business. Ignoring these aspects can lead to financial and legal troubles down the line. In this section, we will explore some of the critical tax and legal considerations that freelancers need to keep in mind.

Subsection 1: Registering Your Business

One of the first things to consider is whether you need to register your business with the local government. Depending on your location and the nature of your work, you may need to obtain a business license, register your business name, or file for a tax ID number. It is crucial to research the requirements in your area and comply with all necessary regulations.

Subsection 2: Understanding Taxes

As a freelancer, you are responsible for paying taxes on your income. It is essential to understand the different types of taxes that may apply to you, such as income tax, self-employment tax, and sales tax. Keep detailed records of your income and expenses, and consult with a tax professional to ensure that you are meeting all tax obligations.

Subsection 3: Deductible Expenses

Freelancers can deduct certain business expenses on their taxes to reduce their taxable income. These may include home office expenses, equipment and supplies, advertising and marketing expenses, and travel expenses related to your business. However, it is essential to keep accurate records and only deduct expenses that are necessary and reasonable.

Subsection 4: Contract and Legal Issues

Freelancers often work on a project-by-project basis, which means that contracts are an essential part of the business. It is essential to have clear contracts with your clients that outline the scope of work, payment terms, and deadlines. Additionally, it is crucial to protect your work and intellectual property by including clauses in your contracts that address ownership and usage rights.

Subsection 5: Insurance

Depending on the nature of your work, you may want to consider obtaining insurance to protect yourself from liability or other risks. Some freelancers may need professional liability insurance or errors and omissions insurance, while others may want to consider general liability insurance or cybersecurity insurance. It is crucial to research your options and obtain the appropriate insurance coverage for your business.

By understanding the tax and legal considerations that come with freelancing, you can ensure that your business is compliant and protected. Taking the time to research and address these issues can save you time, money, and legal headaches in the long run.

Section 3: Managing Your Cash Flow

- Creating a system for invoicing and receiving payments

- Choosing the right payment methods and platforms for your business

- Understanding payment processing fees and how to minimize them

- Creating and following a payment schedule to ensure a steady cash flow

- Managing your accounts receivable and accounts payable to maintain financial stability

One of the most important aspects of running a successful freelance business is managing your cash flow effectively. Cash flow refers to the movement of money in and out of your business, including income from clients, expenses for supplies and equipment, and taxes and other financial obligations.

To manage your cash flow, it's important to have a clear understanding of your income and expenses. This can include tracking your earnings and expenses on a spreadsheet or using a financial management software program.

In addition to tracking your income and expenses, it's also important to have a plan for managing your cash flow over time. This can involve creating a budget, setting financial goals, and regularly reviewing your financial situation to ensure that you are staying on track.

Another key aspect of managing your cash flow is staying on top of your invoices and payments. This can involve sending invoices promptly, following up with clients who are late in paying, and considering options such as accepting partial payments or offering discounts for early payment.

By managing your cash flow effectively, you can ensure that your freelance business remains financially stable and that you are able to meet your financial goals over time. This can involve careful planning, regular monitoring of your finances, and a willingness to adapt and adjust your approach as needed.

Section 4: Building Financial Security

- Creating an emergency fund to protect your business during difficult times

- Saving for retirement and other long-term financial goals

- Choosing the right insurance policies to protect your business and assets

- Understanding how to manage debt and credit effectively

As a freelancer, building financial security should be a top priority. While freelancing can offer the potential for a high income, it can also come with a level of financial instability. Here are some tips for building financial security as a freelancer:

1. Create a budget: Creating a budget is essential for freelancers who want to build financial security. Your budget

should include your expected income, expenses, and savings. Make sure to include both your personal and business expenses in your budget.

2. Save for emergencies: As a freelancer, unexpected events such as a client not paying or a medical emergency can impact your income. It's important to have an emergency fund to help you through these situations. Aim to have three to six months of living expenses saved in an easily accessible account.

3. Diversify your income: Relying on one or two clients can be risky. Look for ways to diversify your income by offering additional services or products, or by finding new clients.

4. Invest in retirement: Freelancers don't have the benefit of employer-provided retirement accounts, but that doesn't mean you shouldn't be investing for retirement. Consider

setting up a solo 401(k) or an individual retirement account (IRA) to help build your retirement savings.

5. Manage debt: While some debt can be helpful, such as business loans to invest in your business, it's important to manage your debt and avoid high-interest credit card debt. Aim to pay off your debts as soon as possible to avoid interest charges.

6. Plan for taxes: As a freelancer, you'll need to pay self-employment taxes. Make sure to set aside a portion of your income for taxes, and consider working with an accountant to make sure you're taking advantage of all available tax deductions.

7. Seek professional advice: Building financial security can be complex, and it can be helpful to seek the advice of a financial planner or accountant who specializes in working with

freelancers. They can help you create a plan to build financial security and provide guidance along the way.

By following the advice and tips in this chapter, you'll be able to manage the financial aspects of your freelancing business with ease and confidence.

Chapter 7: Staying Motivated and Avoiding Burnout

- Tips for staying motivated and productive while working independently
- Strategies for avoiding burnout and maintaining work-life balance
- Ways to stay inspired and engaged in your work as a freelancer

Freelancing on Fiverr can be an exciting and rewarding experience, but it can also be challenging and stressful. In this chapter, we'll explore some strategies to help you stay motivated and avoid burnout, so you can enjoy long-term success as a freelancer.

Section 1: Setting Realistic Goals

- Setting SMART (specific, measurable, achievable, relevant, time-bound) goals to help you stay focused and motivated

- Breaking down larger goals into smaller, manageable tasks

- Celebrating your achievements and progress along the way

- Learning from setbacks and mistakes to improve your performance

One of the keys to success as a freelancer on Fiverr is setting realistic goals. Without clear and achievable goals, it can be difficult to make progress and stay motivated. In this section, we will discuss some strategies for setting realistic goals as a freelancer.

Subsection 1: Understanding Your Limits
Before you can set realistic goals, it's essential to understand your limits as a freelancer. This includes your available time, skills, and resources. By knowing your limits, you can set goals that are challenging but achievable.

Subsection 2: Using the SMART Framework
The SMART framework is an effective way to set realistic goals as a freelancer. SMART stands for Specific, Measurable, Achievable, Relevant, and Time-bound. In this subsection, we will discuss each of these elements and how to apply them to your goal-setting process.

Subsection 3: Breaking Down Larger Goals
Setting larger goals can be daunting, but breaking them down into smaller, more manageable tasks can make them more

achievable. In this subsection, we will discuss how to break down larger goals into smaller, achievable tasks to make progress towards your larger goals.

Subsection 4: Tracking Your Progress Tracking your progress towards your goals is critical to staying motivated as a freelancer. By keeping track of your progress, you can see how far you've come and how much closer you are to achieving your goals. In this subsection, we will discuss some strategies for tracking your progress towards your goals.

Section 2: Maintaining a Work-Life Balance

- Creating a schedule and sticking to it

- Identifying and prioritizing your most important tasks

- Setting boundaries and learning to say "no" to unnecessary work or requests

- Taking breaks and practicing self-care to avoid burnout

As a freelancer on Fiverr, it's easy to blur the lines between work and personal life. Without proper boundaries, it can be challenging to maintain a healthy work-life balance. In this section, we will discuss some strategies for maintaining a healthy work-life balance.

Subsection 1: Setting Boundaries Setting boundaries is critical to maintaining a healthy work-life balance. This includes setting specific work hours, creating a designated workspace, and learning to say no to clients when necessary. In this subsection, we will discuss some strategies for setting boundaries and sticking to them.

Subsection 2: Prioritizing Self-Care Taking care of yourself is crucial to avoiding burnout as a freelancer. Prioritizing self-care means making time for activities that rejuvenate you, such as exercise, hobbies, and spending time with loved ones. In this subsection, we will discuss some strategies for prioritizing self-care and maintaining a healthy work-life balance.

Subsection 3: Managing Time Effectively Effective time management is essential to maintaining a healthy work-life balance. By creating a schedule and sticking to it, you can ensure that you have enough time for work, personal life, and self-care. In this subsection, we will discuss some strategies for managing your time effectively as a freelancer.

Subsection 4: Dealing with Isolation
Freelancing can be a lonely profession, and it's important to take steps to avoid isolation. This includes finding a community of like-minded freelancers, networking, and attending events related to your industry. In this subsection, we will discuss some strategies for dealing with isolation and maintaining a healthy work-life balance.

Section 3: Connecting with Others

- Networking with other freelancers and industry professionals

- Finding a mentor or accountability partner to help you stay on track

- Joining online or in-person communities related to your niche or industry

- Participating in relevant events or conferences to learn and connect with others

Freelancing can be a solitary pursuit, but that doesn't mean you have to go it alone. Connecting with others in your field or in related industries can provide valuable support, networking opportunities, and even potential collaboration.

Here are some ways to connect with others as a freelancer:

1. Join online communities: There are plenty of online communities geared towards freelancers, where you can connect with others in your field, get advice, and even find work. Some popular options include Freelancer's Union, Upwork Community, and Fiverr Forum.

2. Attend industry events: Conferences, workshops, and meetups are great opportunities to connect with other professionals in your field. You can learn from others, share your experiences, and make valuable connections.

3. Reach out to colleagues: If you know other freelancers or professionals in your field, don't be afraid to reach out and connect. You can bounce ideas off each other, collaborate on projects, or simply offer each other support and advice.

4. Collaborate on projects: Working with other freelancers or professionals on a project can be a great way to build relationships and expand your skills. Look for opportunities to collaborate on projects where your skills complement each other.

Remember, building relationships takes time and effort. Be patient, be persistent, and always be open to new connections and opportunities.

Section 4: Continuing to Learn and Grow

- Staying up-to-date with industry trends and best practices

- Seeking out opportunities for professional development and learning

- Experimenting with new skills or services to expand your offerings

- Pursuing certifications or additional education to enhance your credibility and marketability

As a freelancer, it's important to continually learn and grow in your field in order to stay competitive and provide the best possible service to your clients. Here are some tips for continuing your professional development:

1. Take courses and workshops: Whether it's an online course or an in-person workshop, there are plenty of

opportunities to learn new skills and techniques in your field. Look for courses that are taught by industry experts and that offer practical skills you can apply to your work.

2. Read industry publications: Keep up with the latest news and trends in your field by reading industry publications, such as blogs, magazines, and newsletters. This can help you stay informed about new tools, techniques, and best practices.

3. Attend conferences and events: Attending industry events can be a great way to network with others in your field and learn from experts. Look for conferences and events that are relevant to your work and that offer educational sessions and workshops.

4. Seek out mentorship: Finding a mentor who has more experience in

your field can be invaluable for your professional development. A mentor can offer advice, feedback, and guidance as you navigate your career.

5. Practice regularly: Continually practicing and refining your skills is key to improving as a freelancer. Look for opportunities to take on new projects that challenge you and allow you to grow.

Remember, learning and growth are ongoing processes. By committing to your professional development, you can stay up-to-date in your field and continue to provide high-quality services to your clients.

By implementing the strategies outlined in this chapter, you'll be able to maintain your motivation and avoid burnout, so you can continue to grow and succeed as a freelancer on Fiverr.

Chapter 8: Professional Development and Continuing Education

- Opportunities for professional development and education as a freelancer
- How to stay up-to-date with changing trends and technology in your field
- Mentoring and networking opportunities for freelancers

As a freelancer on Fiverr, it's important to stay up-to-date with the latest industry trends and best practices, and to continue to develop your skills and expertise. In this chapter, we'll explore some ways to pursue professional development and continuing education to enhance your knowledge, skills, and marketability.

Section 1: Identifying Your Areas of Improvement

- Assessing your current skills and knowledge gaps

- Identifying areas for improvement based on feedback from clients or peers

- Researching industry trends and new technologies to stay current

As a freelancer, it's important to continually assess your skills and abilities to identify areas where you can improve. By doing so, you can enhance your services, attract more clients, and increase your earnings. This section will explore the process of identifying your areas of improvement and developing a plan to address them.

1.1 Evaluate Your Current Skills and Services

The first step in identifying areas of improvement is to evaluate your current skills and services. Take some time to reflect on your experiences and assess your strengths and weaknesses. Ask yourself the following questions:

- What are my strongest skills and services?

- Which services do I enjoy providing the most?

- Which services have received the most positive feedback from clients?

- Which services have generated the most income?

- Which services have the most competition on Fiverr?

Identifying your strengths and weaknesses can help you focus on areas where you excel and identify areas that need improvement.

1.2 Research the Industry and Competition

After evaluating your current skills and services, research the industry and competition to identify potential areas for improvement. Analyze your competitors' profiles and reviews to see what services they offer and how they differentiate themselves. Additionally, research industry trends to see what services are in high demand and where the industry is headed.

1.3 Develop a Plan to Address Areas of Improvement

Once you've identified potential areas for improvement, develop a plan to address them. Determine the steps needed to improve your skills and services and set realistic goals to achieve them. Consider taking courses, reading books or articles, or seeking advice from other freelancers to help you improve.

1.4 Regularly Assess and Adjust Your Plan

Finally, regularly assess and adjust your plan as needed. As you improve your skills and services, continue to evaluate your progress and adjust your plan accordingly. Set new goals and continue to learn and grow to stay ahead of the competition and provide the best possible services to your clients.

Section 2: Pursuing Formal Education and Certifications

- Considering pursuing a degree or formal certification to enhance your expertise

- Researching educational programs, such as online courses or workshops, to gain new skills or knowledge

- Identifying relevant certifications to demonstrate your proficiency in your niche or industry

While freelancing on Fiverr can offer a great deal of flexibility and independence, it's important to remember that continuing education and certifications can be key to staying competitive and expanding your skillset. Pursuing formal education and certifications can also help you to gain recognition and establish yourself as an expert in your field.

One way to pursue formal education is by taking courses online. There are many reputable online course providers, such as Coursera and Udemy, that offer a wide variety of courses in various fields. These courses can help you to gain new skills and knowledge, and many of them even offer certifications upon completion.

In addition to online courses, there are also many traditional educational programs that can be pursued. This could include earning a degree or certificate from a college or university, or attending a vocational or technical school. While pursuing a traditional education may take more time and resources than taking an online course, it can also provide a more in-depth and comprehensive education.

Another option is to pursue certifications in your field. Certifications are offered by various professional organizations and can demonstrate your expertise in a particular area. For example, if you are a graphic designer, you may consider pursuing certifications such as Adobe Certified Expert or Certified Graphic Designer.

It's important to note that pursuing formal education and certifications can require a significant investment of time and money. Before deciding to pursue a particular course or program, be sure to research the requirements, cost, and potential benefits. Consider speaking with other freelancers or professionals in your field to gain their insight and advice.

Ultimately, pursuing formal education and certifications can help you to stay competitive in the ever-evolving world of freelancing on Fiverr. By continuing to learn and grow, you can expand your skillset, gain recognition, and take your career to the next level.

Section 3: Networking and Collaborating with Other Professionals

- Connecting with other freelancers or industry professionals to learn from their experiences and expertise

- Participating in online or in-person communities to share knowledge and collaborate on projects

- Seeking out mentorship or coaching from experienced professionals in your field

Networking and collaborating with other professionals in your field can be invaluable for your professional development as a freelancer on Fiverr. Not only can it help you learn from others and gain new insights, but it can also open up new opportunities for collaboration and potential clients.

Here are some tips for effective networking and collaboration:

1. Attend industry events and conferences: Attending events and conferences related to your field can be a great way to meet other professionals and learn about new trends and developments in your industry. Look for events both online and in-person that are relevant to your area of work.

2. Join online communities and groups: There are many online communities and groups on social media platforms and forums that are focused on different aspects of freelancing and specific industries. Joining these groups can give you access to valuable information, insights, and potential collaborators.

3. Reach out to other professionals: Don't be afraid to reach out to other

professionals in your field to introduce yourself and start a conversation. You can do this through social media, email, or even by phone. Be respectful of their time and be clear about why you are reaching out to them.

4. Participate in collaborative projects: Collaborating with other professionals on projects can not only help you learn from others, but also showcase your skills and potentially lead to new clients. Look for opportunities to collaborate on projects that align with your skills and interests.

5. Offer your skills to others: One way to build relationships with other professionals is to offer your skills and expertise to help them with their projects. This can be a great way to build rapport and potentially lead to future collaborations.

Remember, effective networking and collaboration takes time and effort, but can be incredibly rewarding for your professional development as a freelancer on Fiverr.

Section 4: Building Your Portfolio and Showcasing Your Expertise

- Continuing to develop and showcase your portfolio with new projects and experiences

- Creating a personal brand and establishing yourself as an expert in your niche or industry

- Seeking out opportunities to share your expertise, such as speaking engagements or guest blog posts

As a freelancer, your portfolio is your best tool for showcasing your skills and expertise to potential clients. Your portfolio should demonstrate your range of abilities and highlight your best work. Here are some tips for building a strong portfolio:

1. Determine your niche: Before you start building your portfolio, it's important to identify your niche. What

type of work do you specialize in? What are your strengths? By identifying your niche, you can tailor your portfolio to showcase your expertise in that area.

2. Select your best work: Your portfolio should feature your best work. Choose a selection of projects that demonstrate your range of skills and highlight your successes. Make sure your portfolio is well-rounded and showcases your abilities in different areas.

3. Use a variety of media: Your portfolio should include a variety of media, such as text, images, and video. Depending on your niche, you may want to include samples of your writing, design work, or video projects.

4. Organize your portfolio: Your portfolio should be easy to navigate and

organized in a way that makes sense. Consider grouping your work by category or type of project. Make sure each project is clearly labeled and includes a brief description.

5. Update your portfolio regularly: Your portfolio should be a living document that you update regularly. As you complete new projects, add them to your portfolio. Make sure your portfolio always reflects your current skills and expertise.

In addition to building a strong portfolio, it's also important to showcase your expertise in other ways. Consider writing blog posts or articles related to your niche, speaking at industry events, or participating in online forums or groups related to your field. These activities can help you establish yourself as an expert in your field and attract new clients to your freelance business.

By pursuing professional development and continuing education, you'll be able to stay ahead of the curve and continue to grow and evolve as a freelancer on Fiverr. This chapter will provide you with the tools and strategies you need to enhance your knowledge, skills, and marketability, and to remain competitive in the ever-evolving world of freelancing.

Chapter 9: Working with International Clients

- Understanding cultural differences and time zone challenges
- Best practices for communicating and working effectively with international clients
- Tools and resources for managing international projects

As a freelancer on Fiverr, you may have the opportunity to work with clients from all over the world. This can be an exciting and profitable experience, but it also presents some unique challenges. In this chapter, we'll discuss how to effectively communicate and work with international clients.

Section 1: Understanding Cultural Differences

Cultural differences can greatly impact the way that clients and freelancers interact. It's important to be aware of these differences and make adjustments to your communication style and work processes as necessary. In this section, we'll explore some of the most common cultural differences you may encounter when working with international clients and how to navigate them.

As a freelancer on Fiverr, you will have the opportunity to work with clients from all over the world. While this can be a great way to expand your business and reach new markets, it also means that you may encounter some cultural differences that can affect how you communicate and work with your clients.

One of the most important things to keep in mind when working with international clients is that cultural norms and expectations can vary widely. What may be acceptable in one culture may not be in another, and it's important to be aware of these differences in order to avoid misunderstandings and communication breakdowns.

For example, in some cultures, direct communication is valued and encouraged, while in others, a more indirect approach is preferred. Similarly, different cultures may have different expectations when it comes to timelines, deadlines, and work schedules.

By taking the time to understand the cultural differences that may impact your work with international clients, you can adapt your communication style and approach to better meet their needs and expectations. This can help you build stronger relationships with your clients and ultimately lead to more successful and profitable collaborations.

Section 2: Communication Strategies

Effective communication is key to successful client relationships, especially when working with clients from different parts of the world. In this section, we'll discuss some communication strategies that can help you bridge the language and cultural barriers that may arise when working with international clients. We'll cover topics such as using clear and concise language, choosing the right communication channels, and managing time zone differences.

When working with international clients, it's important to develop effective communication strategies that take into account cultural differences and language barriers. Here are some tips for communicating effectively with international clients:

1. Use simple language: Avoid using technical jargon or colloquialisms that

may not be understood by clients who speak a different language or come from a different culture. Keep your language simple, concise, and easy to understand.

2. Be mindful of time differences: When working with clients in different time zones, make sure to schedule meetings and deadlines that take into account the time difference. Use tools like world clocks or time zone converters to help you stay organized.

3. Use visuals: Visual aids like diagrams, charts, and graphs can help convey complex ideas and information more effectively than words alone. Use visuals to help bridge any language or cultural barriers.

4. Be respectful of cultural differences: Cultural differences can impact everything from communication styles to business practices. Be respectful of

your clients' culture and try to learn as much as you can about their customs and traditions.

5. Avoid assumptions: Don't make assumptions about your clients based on stereotypes or generalizations. Treat each client as an individual and get to know them on a personal level.

By following these communication strategies, you can build stronger relationships with your international clients and avoid misunderstandings that can impact your work.

Section 3: Legal and Financial Considerations

Working with international clients can also present some legal and financial challenges. In this section, we'll discuss some of the most important considerations you should keep in mind when working with clients from different countries. This includes issues such as payment processing, taxes, and legal agreements.

Working with international clients can have implications beyond just communication and cultural differences. It's important to understand the legal and financial considerations that come with working across borders.

1. Taxation: Depending on the country you're working with, you may need to pay taxes on the income you earn. It's important to research the tax laws in both your home country and the country of your international client to

ensure that you're meeting your obligations.

2. Payment methods: Different countries may prefer different payment methods, so it's important to be familiar with a variety of payment options to accommodate your international clients. Some popular payment methods include PayPal, TransferWise, and international wire transfers.

3. Currency exchange rates: When working with international clients, you'll need to consider currency exchange rates. Make sure you're aware of the current exchange rates, and factor in any fees associated with currency conversion when setting your prices.

4. Legal requirements: Different countries may have different legal requirements for conducting business.

For example, some countries may require you to have a business license or permit in order to operate. Be sure to research the legal requirements of the country you're working with to avoid any legal issues.

5. Intellectual property rights: Intellectual property laws can also vary by country. Make sure you're familiar with the intellectual property laws in both your home country and the country of your international client to ensure that you're not infringing on any copyrights, trademarks, or other intellectual property rights.

By taking the time to understand the legal and financial considerations of working with international clients, you can avoid potential issues and ensure a smooth and successful working relationship.

Section 4: Building Trust and Managing Expectations

Building trust and managing expectations is essential when working with international clients. In this section, we'll discuss some strategies for building trust and establishing clear expectations with clients from different parts of the world. We'll cover topics such as setting clear project milestones, providing regular progress updates, and managing client feedback.

Working with international clients can be a challenge, especially when it comes to building trust and managing expectations. In this section, we will discuss strategies for building trust with international clients and effectively managing their expectations.

One of the keys to building trust with international clients is to be transparent and honest in your communication. It's important to provide clear and concise information about your services, pricing, and timelines, and to be upfront about any potential challenges or delays that may arise. By setting realistic expectations from the beginning, you can avoid misunderstandings and build a strong foundation of trust with your clients.

Another important strategy for building trust with international clients is to be responsive and available. This means being prompt in your communication and making yourself available to answer questions and address concerns. When working with clients in different time zones, it's important to establish clear communication protocols and to be flexible with your schedule.

Managing expectations is also a key component of working with international clients. This involves setting clear boundaries around your availability and the scope of your services, and ensuring that your clients understand what they can expect from you. It's important to be clear about your pricing structure, including any additional fees or charges that may apply, and to provide detailed information about your process and timeline.

Finally, it's important to be mindful of cultural differences when working with international clients. This includes understanding differences in communication styles, business etiquette, and cultural norms. By taking the time to learn about your client's culture and customs, you can build stronger relationships and avoid misunderstandings.

In summary, building trust and managing expectations are critical when working with international clients. By being transparent, responsive, and culturally aware, you can build strong relationships and deliver successful projects.

Working with international clients can be a rewarding experience, but it requires careful planning and communication. By understanding cultural differences, implementing effective communication strategies, and being aware of legal and financial considerations, you can successfully work with clients from all over the world.

Chapter 10: Conclusion and Final Thoughts

- Recap of key takeaways and strategies for success as a freelancer on Fiverr

- Encouragement to keep learning, growing, and taking on new challenges as a freelancer

Congratulations! You've made it to the end of "The Fiverr Freelancer's Handbook: Tips, Tricks, and Strategies for Success." By now, you should have a solid understanding of the world of freelancing on Fiverr and the tools and strategies necessary for success.

In this final chapter, we will wrap up some of the key themes and takeaways from the book, as well as offer some final thoughts and tips for your freelancing journey.

First and foremost, it is important to remember that freelancing on Fiverr is a journey, not a destination. It takes time, effort, and dedication to build a successful career as a freelancer. However, with the right mindset and strategies, you can achieve your goals and enjoy the benefits of a fulfilling and flexible career.

Throughout this book, we have covered a wide range of topics, from setting prices and managing time effectively to building a client base and promoting your services. We've also discussed more advanced topics such as working with international clients and professional development.

As you move forward on your freelancing journey, it's important to remember that there is always room for growth and improvement. Seek out opportunities to learn new skills and expand your knowledge, whether it's through formal education, networking with other professionals, or seeking out mentorship and guidance.

Additionally, remember to take care of yourself and maintain a healthy work-life balance. Freelancing can be both rewarding and challenging, and it's important to find a routine and rhythm that works for you.

Finally, always stay adaptable and flexible. The world of freelancing is constantly evolving, and it's important to be open to new technologies, platforms, and opportunities as they arise. With the right mindset and approach, you can achieve great success as a freelancer on Fiverr.

Thank you for joining us on this journey, and we wish you the best of luck in all your future freelancing endeavors!

www.ingramcontent.com/pod-product-compliance
Lightning Source LLC
LaVergne TN
LVHW051537050326
832903LV00033B/4294